The West

Stephanie

Consultant
Brian Allman
Principal
Upshur County Schools, West Virginia

Publishing Credits
Rachelle Cracchiolo, M.S.Ed., *Publisher*
Emily R. Smith, M.A.Ed., *SVP of Content Development*
Véronique Bos, *VP of Creative*
Dona Herweck Rice, *Senior Content Manager*
Dani Neiley, *Editor*
Fabiola Sepulveda, *Series Graphic Designer*

Image Credits: p10 (top) Photo © North Wind Pictures/Bridgeman Images; p10 (bottom) Library of Congress [LC-DIG-pga-3c13079u]; p12 (top) Library of Congress [LC-DIG-pga-07132]; p12 (bottom) Underwood Archives/UIG/Bridgeman Images; p13 (bottom) Digitally reproduced by the USC Digital Library; From the California Historical Society Collection at the University of Southern California; p14 (top) Library of Congress [2013591597]; p14 (bottom) Time Life Books; p15 Peter Newark Pictures/Bridgeman Images; p17 (top) Library of Congress [LC-DIG-pga-01463]; p17 (bottom) Library of Congress [LC-DIG-pga-08765]; p18 (top) Bridgeman Images; p19 Peter Newark Western Americana/Bridgeman Images; p20 DaTo Images/Bridgeman Images; p21 Alamy Stock Photo/Pictorial Press Ltd; p25 Alaska State Library Historical Collections; p32 Library of Congress [LC-DIG-ppmsca-53150]; all other images from iStock and/or Shutterstock

Library of Congress Cataloging-in-Publication Data
Names: Kraus, Stephanie, author.
Title: The West / Stephanie Kraus.
Description: Huntington Beach, CA : Teacher Created Materials, [2023] | Includes index. | Audience: Grades 4-6 | Summary: "Pack your bags and take a trip out West! Learn about the rich history, diverse cultures, and striking geography of the western United States. It will be clear to see why the West is a popular place to live and visit today"-- Provided by publisher.
Identifiers: LCCN 2022021285 (print) | LCCN 2022021286 (ebook) | ISBN 9781087691053 (paperback) | ISBN 9781087691213 (ebook)
Subjects: LCSH: West (U.S.)--Juvenile literature.
Classification: LCC F591 .K72 2023 (print) | LCC F591 (ebook) | DDC 979--dc23/eng/20220504
LC record available at https://lccn.loc.gov/2022021285
LC ebook record available at https://lccn.loc.gov/2022021286

Shown on the cover is the Big Sur coast in California.

This book may not be reproduced or distributed in any way without prior written consent from the publisher.

5482 Argosy Avenue
Huntington Beach, CA 92649
www.tcmpub.com

ISBN 978-1-0876-9105-3

© 2023 Teacher Created Materials, Inc.

Table of Contents

Welcome to the West 4

A Diverse Landscape 6

Natives of the Land 10

Growing Economies 18

Culture and Daily Life 22

Ready for a Visit? 26

Map It! 28

Glossary 30

Index 31

Learn More! 32

Welcome to the West

Years ago, the western United States might have brought to mind images of cowboys, outlaws, and covered wagons. But what do you picture today? Dry deserts? Miles of farmland? Sunny beaches? Bubbling volcanoes? The answers are endless, and all of them are correct! That is because the region is extremely **diverse**. It is no surprise that it attracts visitors from all around the world. There is something for everyone.

On the Map

Which states make up the West? As it turns out, not all experts agree. In the early days of the United States, it was simple. The West was thought to be anything west of the Appalachian Mountains. This range runs from Canada to Alabama and was seen as a natural border running north to south. In 1803, the United States bought much of the land to the west of it. The deal more than doubled the size of the country. Settlers packed their bags and headed out to the great unknown. Although it was already home to American Indians, people on the East Coast considered it the American frontier.

Hawai'i coast

United States, 1803

Today, there are differing views about which states make up the region. This book will take a closer look at the six states that are farthest west geographically. Come along to explore Alaska, Hawai'i, Washington, Oregon, California, and Nevada.

Long List

In addition to these six states, the United States government also considers six others to be part of the West. These include Arizona, Idaho, Montana, New Mexico, Utah, and Wyoming. Since the West is so vast, it is often broken up into smaller regions, such as the Northwest or the Southwest.

A Diverse Landscape

Juneau, Alaska

The term West Coast is typically used to describe Washington, Oregon, and California. These states border the Pacific Ocean. Some people also think of Alaska and Hawai'i as part of the coast. These two states are often placed near California on a map. However, they are actually thousands of miles from the **mainland**. It takes about five hours to get to Hawai'i from California by plane. Alaska looks like an island on a U.S. map. But it is actually a **peninsula**. It shares its eastern border with Canada.

Big Sur, California

Learning the Climates

Hawai'i is known for its tropical climate. It gets plenty of rain but mainly stays warm and pleasant all year long. The beaches of Hawai'i attract **tourists** no matter the season.

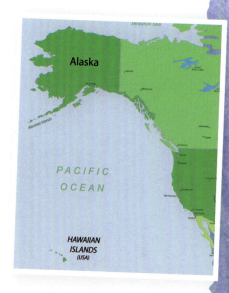

Alaska is almost the exact opposite. It has long, cold winters. It is known for its freezing climate. But summers in parts of Alaska can be sunny and even hot on some days. The state is so far north that in some areas, the sun never sets for about two months in the summer. That means it never rises for a long stretch of time in the winter as well.

Washington and Oregon have a rainy climate. Warm air from the ocean brings heavy rainfall. California's climate varies. It has both cold areas and hot areas as well as both rainy and dry ones. As for Nevada, it is the most **arid** state in the country.

Hot and Cold!

The coldest temperature ever recorded in the United States was in Alaska. It reached –80 degrees Fahrenheit (–62 degrees Celsius)! The hottest temperature ever recorded in the *world* was in Death Valley, California. It hit 134 degrees Fahrenheit (57 degrees Celsius).

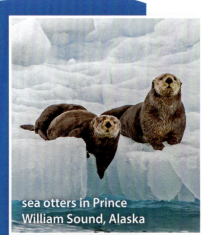

sea otters in Prince William Sound, Alaska

Road Trip Time!

Much of what brings visitors out west are the famous landmarks. None may be more popular than the Grand Canyon. The Colorado River **eroded** the rock around it to reveal deep layers of the earth. The canyon is located in Arizona, but visitors can get to it from the Nevada or Utah border, too. There is even a spot to stand in the three states all at once!

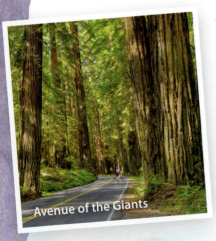
Avenue of the Giants

One of the most popular sites is Yosemite National Park in California. The park's giant rocks were formed thousands of years ago by moving **glaciers**. In the same state, visitors can drive through the Avenue of the Giants. This road winds through towering redwood trees on both sides. In southeast California lies Death Valley. It gets its name from being the lowest, hottest, and driest point in North America.

sand dunes in Death Valley, California

Haleakala volcano crater from the Sliding Sands trail in Maui, Hawai'i

The Columbia River in Oregon is a great place to enjoy the outdoors. It has several waterfalls along the way. Oregon is also home to Crater Lake. The lake was formed by the collapse of a giant volcano. It is the deepest lake in the country.

In Washington, Mount Rainier is a sight to see. The volcano last erupted more than 100 years ago. But it is still active. Mount Rainier is the highest mountain in its range. It is always ice-capped with 25 glaciers running across it. You won't be able to drive there from the mainland, but a boat or plane can get you to Hawai'i's amazing landmarks. Because Hawai'i was formed by volcanoes, a visit to Hawai'i Volcanoes National Park is worthwhile once you arrive. It is one of Hawai'i's most popular spots.

The Tip Top

Denali is a mountain in Alaska that has an elevation of 20,310 feet (6,190 meters). It is the highest peak in North America.

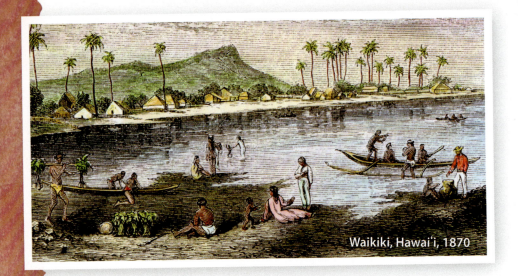
Waikiki, Hawai'i, 1870

Natives of the Land

The first people in Alaska arrived during the Ice Age. Experts think there was a land bridge between Alaska and Asia. Today, that land is under water. Those who settled in the area formed tribes. Many of the tribes are still around.

The Polynesian people were the first to arrive in Hawai'i. They came by boat from the island of Tahiti. Today, they are called Native Hawaiians. Much of the culture there today comes from the native peoples. They have always valued caring for Earth and for one another.

On the West Coast, American Indians lived on the land for more than 10,000 years before Europeans arrived. They built traditions that lasted for centuries. They thrived. Many of the original tribes of the area still exist.

Hupa man catching salmon

Native peoples mainly lived in communities with a social structure. There were leaders among them who decided things for the group as a whole. Groups who lived together were like extended families. They shared resources and culture such as songs, stories, and dances. In the north, they also shared totems. The people of these tribes honored leaders with painted **totem poles**. They were used for other purposes, too. Totem poles were and are important parts of native culture.

In most areas of the West, food was plentiful. This meant that people did not need to spend most of their time finding or hunting food as they might have in other areas. They often shared their resources. In Washington, the native peoples carved canoes out of large trees from the area. They used the canoes to fish for food. On the Nevada and California border, the Washoe peoples lived by beautiful Lake Tahoe. Piñon pine nuts provided food through the long winters there.

piñon pine

About Totem Poles

Totem poles were once carved by hand using simple tools such as stones, bones, and antlers. They were mainly painted black, white, red, and turquoise. The "low man on the totem pole" was actually the most important figure shown. Today's totem poles may be carved with traditional tools. More often, modern axes, carving knives, and even chainsaws are used.

Living with the Land

Where food was plentiful, the people built permanent villages. They could do so because they had natural resources to rely on. The people with more limited resources were more likely to build temporary huts and shelters. They followed food sources and the best climate conditions.

The lives of **Indigenous** peoples in the West varied a great deal depending on the area in which they lived. Climate, landscape, and water supply can make a big difference in shaping people's lives. There was so much diversity across the landscape of the West that there was also great diversity in how the native peoples lived. In fact, in modern-day California alone, there were once more than 100 American Indian tribes. Each had its own culture and lifestyle.

trader in California, 1930

Trade among different groups was common throughout the West. The Chumash peoples of California were well-known for their rich trade culture. Often, they traded seashells and marine animals for animal pelts from the peoples of the Plains.

Indigenous peoples by a stream in Yosemite Valley, California

Living well with the land was a **spiritual** practice for many people of the West. They prayed for there to be plenty from the land and sea. They performed rituals to ensure that they had the best living conditions. They valued taking care of their resources and using only what they needed. This was part of their sacred trust with the land.

Acorns

Acorns grew in abundance in many parts of the West. They were a common food source, especially when ground into flour. They were also sometimes used for trading.

early map of the Baja California peninsula

Spanish Settlement

The native peoples of the West survived and thrived for hundreds of years. Their lives remained mainly unchanged for centuries. Then, Spanish explorers in the 1500s ventured into what would become the American West. Spain was seeking to establish its culture around the world.

Vaqueros

Vaqueros are Spanish cowboys. They took care of the cattle on the ranchos and were often excellent horse riders. Some of the first vaqueros in the area were native peoples.

Spain had already laid claim to many areas throughout Central and South America. Spanish explorers went north from Mexico to Baja California. They began active trade with American Indians farther north. Things continued in this way for about 150 years.

But exploration from other European nations encouraged Spanish explorers to stake a claim beyond Baja. Spanish settlers began to build communities throughout California. Ranchers set up **ranchos** through the West. Many workers on the ranchos were the native peoples. Settlers also formed **pueblos**. The pueblos were heavily armed, mainly in defense against the native peoples of the area. The people fought back as settlers took their land and resources.

The Catholic Church in Spain also played a strong role in the development of the West during this time. Catholic **missionaries** were sent to build 21 missions up the Pacific coast. Spain had two main goals for the missionaries. The first was to convert the native peoples to Catholicism. The second was to expand Spain's hold and to keep the native peoples under control. Many of these people were forced into labor at the missions.

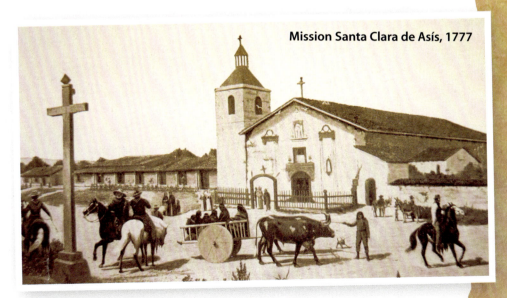

Mission Santa Clara de Asís, 1777

U.S. Claim

There were growing challenges for the native peoples as more and more settlers arrived. The newcomers claimed native lands. The trickle of settlers soon became a stream, and the stream became a rushing current. Explorers, settlers, and missionaries grew in power. In time, there was little the native peoples could do to stop the flood of change and control.

In the 1800s, the United States turned its attention to westward expansion. The nation encouraged its people to travel west. In 1803, President Thomas Jefferson purchased a massive area of westward land for $15 million from France. Known as the Louisiana Purchase, it about doubled the size of the country. Then, the United States went to war with Mexico, which owned the land under Spanish rule. The Mexican-American war began in 1846. The nations fought over the Texas and Mexico border. But the United States quickly took control of Mexico City. Mexican leaders decided to make a deal. They sold the land that today makes up California, Nevada, Utah, Arizona, New Mexico, and more to the United States. The United States paid $15 million for the purchase. Mexico lost about half its land.

Battle of Palo Alto, Mexican-American War

California boomtown

The Gold Rush

Days before the war ended, gold was discovered in California. This started one of the largest gold rushes in history. Thousands of people moved to California to strike it rich. The next year, 80,000 people came in search of gold.

Miners spent their days searching through rocks to find gold. Most miners found no gold at all. People also moved west to sell supplies to the miners. Experts say those suppliers likely made more money than most of the miners.

When a miner did find gold in an area, word spread quickly. Others would move in and set up camp. The new areas were called *boomtowns*. Boomtowns also sprang up in Nevada, but they were for silver mining.

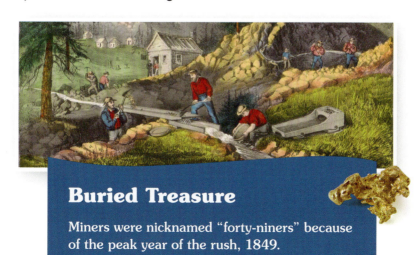

Buried Treasure

Miners were nicknamed "forty-niners" because of the peak year of the rush, 1849.

fur trading

Growing Economies

The economy of the West has, of course, changed a lot over time. Native peoples mainly found or made their own resources and traded for other goods they needed. They provided services among their own communities. Everyone had roles to play.

As others moved into the area, they first developed a fur trade. This was the main industry in the western mainland for over 300 years. American Indians traded animal furs to settlers in exchange for weapons and tools. The settlers then sold the furs to be used for clothing and hats. The state of Oregon's nickname even comes from fur trading. It is called the Beaver State.

Cattle ranching was also popular at that time. Cattle owners often lived on big properties without any fencing. They hired cowboys to herd their cattle. They took the animals to market to be sold. Today, most ranches are smaller and fenced in. That means there are fewer cowboys today.

In the early 1900s, Washington was number one in timber production. Oregon eventually took that title. Forests cover almost 50 percent of Oregon. There are many shipping ports in both states. The ports make it easier to ship wood around the world. Many lumber companies are still based in the Northwest.

In the 1800s, sugar farms became popular in Hawai'i. The soil is also good for growing coffee and pineapples. Hawai'i exports a lot of these goods throughout the United States and the world. Alaska is known for its fresh seafood. Seafood is Alaska's top export.

Entertainment in the Wild West

William "Buffalo Bill" Cody was an American soldier, bison hunter, and showman. He organized Wild West shows with cowboys and sharpshooters. Annie Oakley was one of the show's top performers. She developed her shooting skills as a child to provide food for her hungry family.

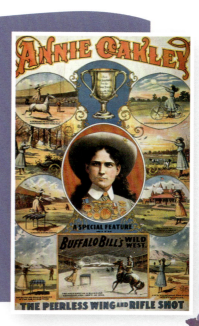

Be Our Guest

Many Western states want tourists to come visit. When people vacation, they spend money at hotels, restaurants, and shops. This brings money to the states. It also creates jobs for the locals.

Las Vegas is one of the most popular tourist destinations in the world. The city is located in a desert in Nevada. People come from all over the world for its casinos, hotels, restaurants, and entertainment. Talented performers draw tourists to spectacular shows.

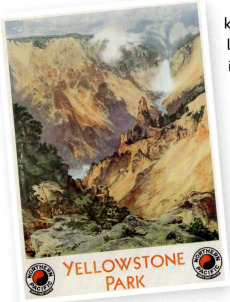

California started out as a state known for farming. It still has a large farming industry. But today, it is celebrated for much more. It is home to popular tourist destinations such as Disneyland and the San Diego Zoo. Both are top spots for family vacations. And many TV shows and movies are filmed in Los Angeles. People visit in hopes of seeing celebrities and movie sites.

Las Vegas, Nevada

Helicopter tours are popular in Hawai'i and Alaska. In Alaska, travelers can see icy mountain glaciers from the sky. Sightseers can also go whale watching in Alaska. They can learn about fishing from the locals. In Hawai'i, tourists can look down into volcanoes. Visitors can also pay to attend a **luau**. The celebration honors native Hawaiian culture.

And who could forget the beaches? One of the top reasons people visit the West is to go to the beautiful beaches. They may want to surf big waves or just relax on the sand.

Bright Lights

The city of Las Vegas has millions of lights that dazzle its skyline. It is considered the brightest spot on Earth and can even be seen from space.

Culture and Daily Life

The culture of the West is popularly known for being casual and "laid back." Compared to the East Coast, many people say that the West Coast has a slower pace of life. Even the way of speaking is considered slower in the West.

Hawai'i is known for being mellow and relaxed. People there are said to embrace the **aloha** spirit. It focuses on love, respect, and working together. Research shows that residents of Hawai'i live longer than in any other state.

Portland is the most populated city in Oregon. Residents there are known for caring about the environment. Seattle is a bustling town in Washington. It has great art and attractions. It is known for culture—and coffee! But it is sometimes thought of as gloomy because of all the rain it gets.

Los Angeles, California, is known for being sunny and glamorous. That is mostly because of **affluent** areas such as Hollywood and Beverly Hills. These areas are where movie stars live and work.

When people think of Alaska, they tend to think of **igloos** and polar bears. While those do exist, they are not common in everyday life. Igloos were more commonly used in the past. Visiting beautiful outdoor settings, hiking, fishing, and hunting are popular in Alaska.

a cafe in Kauai, Hawai'i

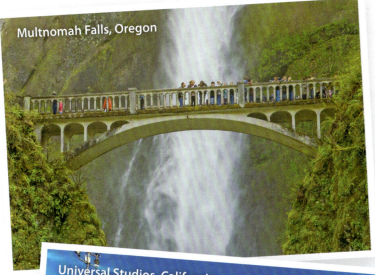
Multnomah Falls, Oregon

Universal Studios, California

Juneau, Alaska

Civics

As is true anywhere in the United States, the West is run by the people. People decide on their leaders. They elect their mayors, council members, and state governors. They cast votes on tax measures and propositions. Together, they have a big say in how things are done.

Some people throughout the West tend to be very involved in their civic lives. They get behind endeavors that matter to them. Throughout much of the West, one of the greatest concerns is the environment. From Alaska to Hawai'i to the southern tip of California, people are very involved in both protecting and making use of the natural resources. They vote, take office, and hold protests to let their voices be heard.

Western states are among the newest in the nation. California is the oldest state among these six Western states. It joined the United States in 1850. Oregon was next to join in 1859. Then came Nevada in 1864 and Washington in 1889. Alaska and Hawai'i did not become states until the 1900s. They are the two most recent states to become part of the United States. Alaska joined in January 1959. Hawai'i entered the union in August of that same year.

Leader from the West

In 2021, Kamala Harris became the vice president. She is a Democrat from California. Harris is the first female vice president of the country. She is also the first Black and first Asian American person to hold the title. Many people on the West Coast voted for her.

Major cities in the West have great influence on what is done throughout the region. Los Angeles is at the center of many issues. Experts say the city has a large impact on the voting in nearby states. Seattle, Portland, and San Francisco are other influential cities throughout the West.

Alaska and Hawaii Statehood

After 125 Years Girl Born at Last In Lott Family

ERIE, Pa., (UP) — For the first time in the past 125 years a girl has been born in the Lott family.

It happened last night at the M. D. General Hspital in nearby Lawrence Park when Mrs. Delbert Lott of Millcreek gave birth to a girl whom they named Cindy.

Lott, production manager of the Zurn Manufacturing Co., said 20 boys had been born in his family over the past 125 years, but nary a girl until Cindy came along.

Principal's Job 'Too Much;' Prefers Teaching History

SPARKS, Nev., (UP) — Edwin Whitehead resigned last week as principal of Sparks High School but will remain as a history teacher.

"That job was too much to worry about," said Whitehead, who will take a drop in pay from $7,600 to $6,500 a year.

Dist. school supt. Earl Wooster said he could understand.

"In a job like his, you're never right, and catch it from the school board, parents, pupils and newspapers," Wooster explained.

GIRL SCOUT NEWS
Troop 66 Rose Brownies

Five Brownies were present the day of our meeting. We are painting our puppet's heads and putting the aair on our puppets. We are also finishing the puppet play about Rose Red and Snow White. Miss Ross gave us each a stick of candy and then the meeting was dismissed.

Scribe, Linda Lenert.

RECEPTION PLANNED FOR EPISCOPAL BISHOP ARRIVING HERE TOMORROW

The Right Reverend William Gordon Jr., Bishop of the Episopal Church in Alaska, accompanied by Rev. Alvin Reiners Jr. of Kotzebue, will arrive in Nome Tuesday.

Following the church services, an informal reception honoring the visiting clergymen will be hled at the home of Mr. and Mrs. Russell R. Hermann. Assisting Mrs. Hermann will be Mrs. Robert Grant, Mrs. Phillip Dexter and Mrs. Russell Hardy.

· BRING YOUR
WATCH

Communism Is An Issue, Says House Group Chairman

By FRANK W. VAILLE

WASHINGTON, (UP) — The chairman of a Congressional committee that is handling Alaska statehood bills says he "fully intends to end a hearing on the bills by April 6.

Chairman O'Brien (D-N. Y.) of the House Territories Subcommittee made this statement Friday in winding up the first week of the hearing, which he recessed until Wednesday.

The April 6 date is two days before the subcommittee is scheduled to take up similar bills that would grant statehood to Hawaii.

O'Brien told a witness yesterday that he decided to support separate consideration of the Alaska and Hawaii statehood bills partly because of the Communism issue.

The witness, Dr. P. Gordon Gould of Philadelphia, a native of Unga, Alaska, had testified that he had never met an Alaskan who favored Communism.

O'Brien said that when joint consideration was given two years ago to statehood for Alaska and Hawaii, almost all the arguments were directed "at alleged Communist tendencies of certain unions in Hawaii" with no relation to the merits of Alaskan statehood. The House defeated that bill.

Gould, a minister, now is giving full time to helping establish the Alaska Methodist University at Anchorage. He said statehood should be granted Alaska because "stateside public opinion favors it," because the caliber of its citizens "warrants" it, and because its strategic location could make Alaska a show window for democracy.

Alice Stuart of Fairbanks, who identified herself as editor and published of a "photo-memo book" called the "Alaska Calendar for Engagements," testified against the bills. She expressed belief a majority of Alaskans would oppose statehood now if given the opportunity to vote on it.

All Alaskans "want statehood someday when we can afford it," she said. Alaskans have never been given an opportunity to "vote on the bills-eye question" of immediate statehood, she said.

O'Brien said she had offered no evidence to support her contention. Referring to his advo-

much friction."

She said a 1946 referendum on statehood, in which advocates prevailed 9,630 to 6,822, was on the general subject of statehood rather than on the question of immediate statehood.

A. M. Buddy, president of the Alaska Sportsmen's Council, suggested an amendment to the statehood bill directing that commercial fisheries be managed by a separate agency than sports fisheries and wildlife. He said the Alaska Legislature had put the two under a commission "dominated by commercial fishing interests."

O'Brien then said that was a matter which should be left to the Legislature and one which was not "pertinent to statehood."

Buddy then said that he also questioned the advisability of including within the statehood bill the withdrawal authority recommended by the administration.

He said he believed this authority, under which the President could set up military reservations in northern and western Alaska, would be detrimental to resources development.

Industry, he said, would be reluctant to invest money in an area threatened by possible withdrawals.

O'Brien said he shared Buddy's concern on this score, but added that from a "practical" standpoint, the withdrawal proposal was a compromise under which immediate statehood would receive administration backing.

"It's a handicap to statehood," O'Brien said, "but without it we haven't a chance."

Scheduled to testify later are "Rep." Ralph J. Rivers of Fairbanks, Mike Erceg, Fairbanks; Mrs. R. I. C. Prout, president of the General Federation of Women's Clubs; Francis O. Wilcox, Assistant Secretary of State; Charles Callison, National Wildlife Federation, and C. R. Gutermuhh, Wildlife Management Institute.

BIBLE READINGS —
for use during
Lent and Easter, 1957

MARCH

Friday 8 .... Romans 8:31-39
Saturday 9 .... II Timothy 2:7-15
Sunday 10 .... Psalm 51:1-13
Monday 11 .... Luke 10:25-37

A newspaper announces the new states of Alaska and Hawai'i.

Ready for a Visit?

Like most of the country, the West has a complex and interesting past. Today looks so different from how it did years before. Instead of ranches and missions, the West now has tourism, business, filmmaking, and more.

There is much to explore out West. The varying climates and cultures make each state unique. From farms and beaches to national parks and volcanoes, it's easy to see why tourism is growing! Whether someone is looking for quiet, untouched land or a bustling city of lights, the West has just the spot. The attractions are as diverse as the people who live there. Landmarks serve as daily reminders of the deep history rooted in this region.

Each day, cities grow more populated. New industries are created. We can see why the West is so often shown in TV shows and movies. The charm and beauty shine on screen, just as they do in real life.

Portland, Oregon

Los Angeles, California

Seattle, Washington

State Nicknames

Every state has an official nickname.
Here are the nicknames of the states of the West:
Alaska: Last Frontier
California: Golden State
Hawai'i: Aloha State
Nevada: Silver State
Oregon: Beaver State
Washington: Evergreen State

Map It!

The West is an area rich with natural resources. Natural resources are materials that occur in nature. Some examples of natural resources are air, water, sunlight, and plants. Human-made resources are items that have value to humans but do not occur in nature. Some examples of human-made resources are homes, cars, and roads.

Make a map to show the natural resources of the West. Follow these steps to create your map:

1. Research to learn about the West's major natural resources and how they contribute to the area's economy.
2. Draw a map outline of the West and its states.
3. Add symbols on the map for the natural resources, drawing them in the major areas where they can be found.
4. Add a map key to tell what each symbol stands for.
5. Share your map. Be prepared to explain how each natural resource brings money to the West.

Glacier Bay National Park, Alaska

brown bears in Alaska

Kamiak Butte County Park, Washington

Honolulu, Hawai'i

Glossary

affluent—having a great deal of money; wealthy

aloha—the Hawaiian word for hello, love, and peace

arid—dry

cattle ranching—raising cows on a large farm, usually for food

diverse—made up of people or things that are different from one another

eroded—gradually worn away

glaciers—slow-moving masses or rivers of ice

igloos—dome-shaped shelters built from blocks of solid snow

Indigenous—from or native to a particular area

luau—a Hawaiian feast

mainland—a large area of land that forms a country without any islands included

missionaries—people who travel to a foreign country to do religious work

peninsula—a piece of land surrounded by water on three sides

pueblos—towns of Spanish or Mexican origin

ranchos—large land grants given to people as favors from Spanish or Mexican leaders that are mainly used for raising cattle and sheep

spiritual—relating to religion or religious beliefs

totem poles—wooden monuments carved and painted with symbols

tourists—travel to or visit a place for vacation or pleasure

Index

American Indians, 4, 10–18

Appalachian Mountains, 4

Colorado River, 8

Columbia River, 9

cowboys (vaqueros), 4, 14, 18–19

Death Valley, 7–8

Denali, 9

Disneyland, 20

fish, 10, 11, 21

gold rush, 17

Harris, Kamala, 24

Hawai'i Volcanoes National Park, 9

Lake Tahoe, 11

Las Vegas, 20–21

Louisiana Purchase, 16

Mexican-American War, 16

missions, 15, 26

Mount Rainier, 9

Polynesian, 10

ranches (ranchos), 14–15, 18, 26

San Diego Zoo, 20

Spain, 14–15

totem poles, 11

West Coast, 6–7, 10–11, 22–25

Yosemite National Park, 8

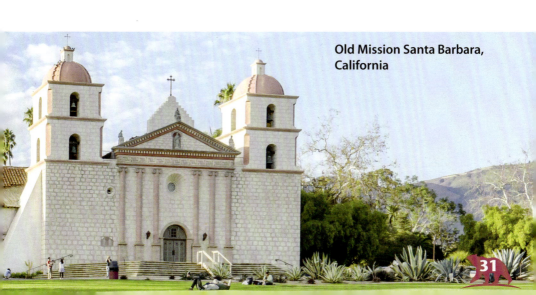

Old Mission Santa Barbara, California

Learn More!

For many years, native peoples lived and thrived throughout the West. They had rich cultures and ways of life.

- Research the native tribes of the West, and select one of their leaders.

- Learn more about that leader and what they did to lead their people. Were they a successful leader? What made them great? Why should they be remembered?

- Make a poster to show the highlights of this leader's life. Include an illustration of the leader.

O'ahu, Hawai'i

Queen Lili'uokalani